CONTENTS

THE CHURCH AND THE MEDIEVAL AGE

Pope Adrian IV
Adrian IV was the only Englishman who became a pope. Here, a friend recalls how difficult it was for him to do the job:
'He used to say that no one is more wretched than the Roman pontiff [the pope]....
Even if he had no other problems, the weight of his duties alone would overwhelm him. He confided to me that he had found so many cares in the cathedral of Peter [in Rome] that by comparison all his earlier troubles seemed like joyful moments and happy times. He added that were it not for fear of opposing the decision of God he would have preferred never to have left his native England....'
(*From* Medieval Worlds: A Sourcebook, *edited by Roberta Anderson and Dominic Bellenger*)

The extent of Christianity by the twelfth century CE.

Christianity is a religion that follows the teachings of Jesus Christ, a man who lived in Palestine two thousand years ago. At that time, Palestine was a part of the Roman Empire. Today, there are many different branches of Christianity, but in the medieval age most of these had not yet developed. Christianity in the medieval age meant the Church, and it was an essential part of life for people throughout Europe.

Across the Roman Empire, in the centuries after the death of Christ, usually given as 30 or 33 CE, the numbers of his followers had grown slowly. At that time, the Roman Empire extended from England in the north to parts of northern Africa in the south, and from Spain in the west to what is now Iraq in the east. At first, though there were groups of Christians in the major cities of the Roman Empire, there was no central organization to the Church. However, the religion gradually developed its influence until, by the tenth century, the Church had become a wealthy and powerful institution, ruled by men called bishops.

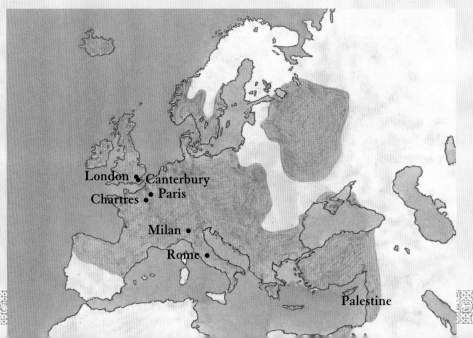

London • Canterbury
Chartres • • Paris

Milan •

Rome •

Palestine

Medieval
World

EDRALS

CHURCH

CIA LEVY

W
FRANKLIN

This edition printed in 2006

First published in 2004 by
Franklin Watts
338 Euston Road, London NW1 3BH

Franklin Watts Australia
Hachette Children's Books
Level 17/207 Kent Street, Sydney, NSW 2000

Produced by Arcturus Publishing Limited,
26/27 Bickels Yard, 151-153 Bermondsey Street, London SE1 3HA.

© 2004 Arcturus Publishing Limited

Editor: Clare Weaver
Designer: Chris Halls, Mind's Eye Design Ltd, Lewes
Illustrator: Adam Hook
Picture researcher: Glass Onion Pictures

A CIP catalogue record for this book is available from the British Library.

ISBN-13: 978 0 7496 6988 1
ISBN-10: 0 7496 6988 8

Dewey Decimal Classification Number: 726.6'0902

Printed and bound in China

Picture Acknowledgements: Akg-images/Schutze/Rodemann 21; The Art
Archive/Bibliotheque Municipale Reims/Dagli Orti 5/Musee des Arts Decoratifs
Paris/Dagli Orti (A) 7/University Library Prague/Dagli Orti 9/Dagli Orti 10,
19/Canterbury Cathedral/Dagli Orti (A) 14/Bodleian Library, Oxford 20/Bodleian
Library Oxford, Canon Class lat 81 folio 137r 17/British Library 22/Canterbury
Cathedral/Jarrold Publishing 27/The Art Archive 28/Galleria deli Uffizi
Florence/Dagli Orti (A) 29; Bibliotheque Nationale, Paris 12; Bodleian Library,
Oxford MS.Bodl.264, pt.1 24; The British Library/HIP 13; Topham Picturepoint 23.

Prologue ca geftes des Roys De france

m cefte semue comence Astoire   longue parole et confuse

The Church was involved in almost every aspect of life in the Middle Ages, from regulating the daily conduct of the people to investing a king. Here, bishops crown the king of France.

Ecclesiastical Courts

The Church in Rome operated its own courts, known as ecclesiastical courts. Church laws governed most people's lives just as much as the general laws of their country did. Church law covered marriage, the care of children, usury (the lending of money for a fixed charge), legal contracts that involved the taking of an oath, and the payment of special taxes to the Church, called tithes. The Church could punish people with fines or physical punishment; it could also expel wrongdoers from the Church – a very serious punishment called excommunication.

The central organization of the Church was in Rome. The bishop of Rome was, and still is, called the pope and he became the leader of the other bishops. The pope made all the final decisions about matters to do with the Church. He also had a special power to release people from the consequences of committing sins (breaking the laws of the Church). Sins could include general crimes, like murder, as well as special Church crimes like heresy, the refusal to accept the teachings of the Church.

Each of the old regions of the Roman Empire, which had begun to break up in Europe in the fifth century, had its own bishop. The bishops based themselves in large churches in the major town of the region, or diocese, they were responsible for. Each diocese was split up into parishes, served by smaller churches. The more powerful bishops, based in the larger and more important towns, became known as archbishops. Some bishops also held the higher rank of cardinal. Cardinals helped to decide who was to be pope.

CHANGES IN THE CHURCH

Church Building

For about three hundred years, from the beginning of the eleventh century, a wave of church building took place throughout Europe. Cathedrals, special churches where a bishop was in charge, became bigger, and new parish churches were built. Many of these buildings no longer exist, but it is known that from 1050 to 1350, eighty cathedrals, five hundred large churches, and tens of thousands of parish churches were built in France alone – one church for every two hundred people. The French quarried several million tons of stone to build these religious structures, more stone than the ancient Egyptians had used throughout the centuries of pyramid building.

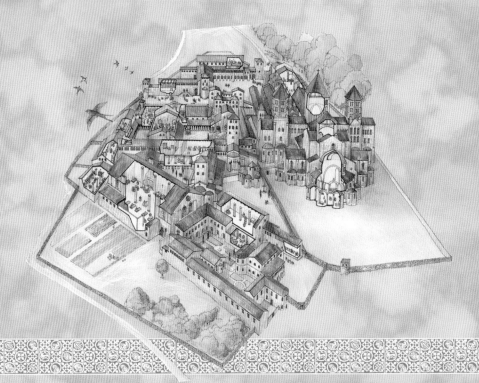

A bird's-eye view of the large, self-contained Benedictine monastery at Cluny in France.

Because the Church was so influential, powerful people fought for control of it. Until the eleventh century, bishops, and even the pope himself, were often chosen by kings. This meant that the king could appoint a bishop who would do what he was told, and the king could control what happened to church incomes. Another problem that many Church leaders faced was corruption within the Church. As the Church became richer, popes failed to establish firm rules for the behaviour of Church leaders. Bishops became very wealthy and powerful men who enjoyed privileged lives. In 1073, the new pope, Gregory VII, had very strong views about the way in which the clergy should conduct their lives, and about who should appoint the bishops and other clergymen. From the time of Gregory's rule, Church leaders were usually appointed by the pope or by a group of cardinals. The bishops in their turn appointed the parish priests and other clergymen who worked for them. This meant that the Church had better

An influential man, with sincerely held views about the role of the Church, Pope Gregory VII had an enormous influence on the Church for generations. Here he is shown blessing King Henry IV of Germany.

A Lordly Bishop
A contemporary clergyman disapproves of a corrupt bishop:
'This Anthony Bek [1283-1311] was second to none in the realm, save the king only, in pomp and bearing and might of war, busy rather about the affairs of kingdom than of his diocese, a powerful ally to the king ... to him it was a small thing that the greatest earls and barons ... should kneel before him, or that, while he remained seated knights should stand long and tediously before him like servants. Nothing was too dear for him if only it should magnify his glory. He bought cloth of the rarest and costliest and made it into horse cloths ... he was never in want and abounded in all things unto the day of his death.'
(*From* Life in the Middle Ages, *G. C. Coulton*)

control of its own money and this gave it more independence. Gregory also decided that clergymen should not marry, and he laid down strict rules of behaviour for them.

Gregory's reforms led to other important developments within the Church. Since the early years of Christianity, people who felt very close to their religion had joined monasteries, places that were isolated from society where they could dedicate themselves to worship. Monasteries became more organized in the sixth century, under the influence of St Benedict. He imposed rules on the monasteries he founded: monks had to study and pray for set periods each day. After Pope Gregory's changes, many more monasteries were founded. The reforms not only gave monasteries greater freedom from the interference of kings, but also encouraged many ordinary people to take up the monastic life.

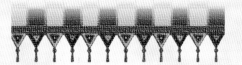

THE CHURCH AND SOCIETY

Pope Urban's Speech to the Knights of Europe:

'If you wish to be mindful of your souls, advance boldly, as knights of Christ, and rush as quickly as you can to the defence of the Eastern Church.... Under Jesus Christ, our Leader, may you struggle for your Jerusalem, in Christian battle line … that you may assail and drive out the Turks … and may you deem it a beautiful thing to die for Christ in that city in which He died for us. But if it befall you to die this side of it, be sure that to have died on the way is of equal value, if Christ shall find you in His army. God pays with the same shilling, whether at the first or eleventh hour.'
(*From* The First Crusade: The Accounts of Eyewitnesses and Participants, *August C. Krey*)

A Crusader sets off for the Holy Land, ready to give up his life for the Church.

It is difficult for us today to understand just how important the Church was to ordinary people in the medieval age. From birth onwards, people's lives were governed by the Church. Clergymen (Church officials) baptised infants, controlled the education of children, performed marriage services, and when someone died, they supervised their burial and conducted prayers for their soul.

People generally believed that their behaviour while they were alive would determine their destination after death. They thought that those people who died without committing

Jan Hus (c. 1369–1415), a peasant from Bohemia, campaigned against Church corruption and was burned at the stake as a heretic. His death inspired his followers, the Hussites, to take up arms, and war raged in Bohemia until 1434.

Heresy

Besides Muslims (also called Saracens), there were other people, called heretics, who were seen as a threat to medieval Christianity. Heretics were Christians who questioned whether certain Church beliefs and teachings were true. One such group were the Cathars, who believed that everything material – wealth, property, even everyday necessities – was evil. The Hussites were another group who refused to recognize the authority of the Pope, or that only priests could carry out the important religious services. In the early medieval period heretical groups were generally tolerated. However, from the thirteenth century, heretics were persecuted by a special court known as the Inquisition, and hundreds of people were burned to death for heresy.

any sins would go to heaven, while those who died without seeking forgiveness would go to hell. They also believed that confessing their sins and asking for forgiveness would grant them a shorter stay in purgatory, a place where those who died went in order to pay for sins that they had confessed to while they were alive.

One way in which people thought that they could reduce their time in purgatory was to contribute money to the Church. Rich men, including kings, noblemen and merchants, provided the money to build magnificent cathedrals. They did this to pay for their sins and also gain power and influence while they were alive.

The power of the Church was demonstrated in 1095 by the launch of the Crusades. This was a series of military expeditions made by European Christians to retake Palestine, a land sacred to Christians and at that time under Muslim control. Pope Urban II made a speech urging Christian knights to take back the Holy Land. Thousands of men of all classes set off to fight, many of them never to return. They believed that what they were doing was the will of God and that taking part would guarantee their place in heaven.

CHURCH BUSINESS

The Importance of Holy Relics

Holy relics were highly prized items in medieval times. A really wealthy man, such as a king or baron, might have his own personal collection, and churches kept their collections securely locked up. The relic might be the entire remains of a saint or just a fragment of their finger bone, the water a saint's corpse might have been washed in, or a fragment of what was claimed to be the cross on which Christ was crucified. One medieval source tells the story of St Hugh of Lincoln, who attempted to steal part of a relic from a monastery in France by biting off a piece of the finger of a female saint.

Churches before the medieval age were places where ordinary people tended to go only at Easter, when they were expected to confess their sins and take part in a ritual called communion. The growth of religious belief in the medieval age changed all that. Churches became the heart of the community.

The medieval Church was very much involved in the daily lives of its parishioners. The parish priest was expected to supervise a number of rituals – listening to confession, baptizing babies, blessing marriages, confirming the faith of young people, providing spiritual aid to the dying and overseeing the burial of the dead. Everyone was expected to attend the ceremony called mass, which took place on Sundays. The Church was also the main source of education for ordinary people. People learned bible stories from stone carvings and the paintings that decorated church walls. People were taught the penalties of sin and told they would be judged by God after they died.

In the San Guiliano Convent in Italy are the relics (cloak and purse) of St John of Capistrano (1386–1456).

These pilgrims visit the shrine of a saint, perhaps to ask a cure for an illness. They collected badges at each shrine they visited in order to display their piety.

The Value of a Relic
This passage describes the efforts of people to get a piece of the clothes of a dead saint as her body is carried to the church for burial:
'The whole people flocked together and rushed upon the sacred body with incredible ardour so that the guards could by no means keep them at arm's length. Before the procession had reached the church three tunics had been cast upon her for each in turn was cut into pieces.... The soldiers who did all they might to defend her with swords and maces, could scarce hinder the people from cutting her body itself into pieces in their excess of devotion.'
(*From* Life in the Middle Ages, *C. G. Coulton*)

The Church year began with the twelve days of Christmas, celebrating the birth of Christ. This festival was followed by Shrovetide, and then Holy Week. This commemorated the death of Christ and was the most important religious event of the year. Church processions took place and everyone was expected to take part in the ritual called Holy Communion. Summer was marked in the Christian calendar by Corpus Christi, a celebration of the Church belief that Christ was bodily present in the bread taken at mass. This was also accompanied by religious processions. Finally, the year ended with All Souls and All Hallows, when the Church held prayers for the souls of the dead.

Another big business for the Church, especially in the cathedrals and grand town churches, was pilgrimages. In medieval times, people believed they could be cured of illness if they touched a holy relic. Pilgrims to a shrine that contained the relic of a saint would donate money to the church in exchange for a cure. On a particular saint's day, the church holding a relic of the saint would be crowded with pilgrims.

A PEOPLE'S CHURCH

Marriage

In early medieval times, the Church was not involved in the marriage contract, but people usually exchanged their promises of loyalty at the front door of their local church. After these exchanges, they attended a mass inside the church. In 1200, the Church in England ordered that in future the priest should be present at the exchange of vows:
'And let not any marriage be contracted unless there is a threefold proclamation in the church, nor if the persons are not known. And let persons not be joined in matrimony unless publicly in the face of the church with a priest present. If it is done otherwise, let them not be admitted anywhere in church without special permission of the bishop.'
(From Medieval Worlds: A Sourcebook, *edited by Roberta Anderson and Dominic Bellenger)*

Here, some time around 1400, the Bishop of Paris blesses the fair at Lendit, near to the city.

Besides the official role of the Church in the lives of the ordinary people, there were other more practical matters expected of the priest. He was often the only person in the parish who could read and write, and many priests set up informal schools to teach young children. The priest might also use his literacy skills to assist with the legal problems of his parishioners. He would be called upon to settle disputes, bless the crops and administer the business of collecting tithes.

In many country areas the parish church may well have been the only building of any substance, and probably the only one built of stone. In cities, the cathedral was as much a meeting place as it was a place of worship. The main body, or nave, of the church (where today there are rows of benches for the congregation) was unfurnished in medieval times. This provided a big, multipurpose, open space. Guilds, which were trade or craft associations, held their meetings in their local

An important part of the job of a Church leader in the Middle Ages was to bring converts into the Church. Here an adult is welcomed into the faith through baptism. Those born into Christian families were baptised shortly after birth.

church. We know that banquets were held in cathedrals because, in 1358, they were banned in an English cathedral after complaints about excessive eating. Mystery plays – stories about the life of Christ – were performed in many churches at Christmas and Easter.

Some cathedrals were even used for fairs or markets. At Troyes in France, month-long champagne markets were held around the city's churches, and goods were put into the church store-rooms for safe keeping. Salisbury Cathedral in England hosted for a time a horse fair, both in the churchyard and in the building itself. Even St Paul's Cathedral in London was, in the fourteenth century, used as a marketplace and as a place for drawing up legal contracts. All over Europe it was common at harvest times to use the parish church for threshing the corn and, later, for storing it.

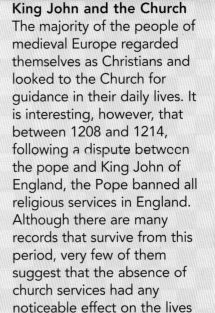

King John and the Church
The majority of the people of medieval Europe regarded themselves as Christians and looked to the Church for guidance in their daily lives. It is interesting, however, that between 1208 and 1214, following a dispute between the pope and King John of England, the Pope banned all religious services in England. Although there are many records that survive from this period, very few of them suggest that the absence of church services had any noticeable effect on the lives of ordinary people.

CATHEDRALS

Some Cathedral Terms

The *nave* is the central area of the church where the congregations stood in medieval times.

The *chancel* is the eastern end of the church where the priests and the choir stand. It is divided off from the nave.

An *apse* is a circular extension on the main body of the church. It often holds a private chapel. In early churches the chancel was a simple apse.

The *clerestory* is a series of ornate windows on the first floor of the nave, above the roof of the aisle. It allows light into the body of the church, through elaborate and beautiful stained glass windows.

The *transept* is an aisle, which crosses the church at the east end in front of the chancel. In Gothic churches it extends into two extra rooms at the north and south of the church, making the building cross-shaped.

A thirteenth-century stained glass window from Canterbury Cathedral.

The Church in medieval Europe was divided into administrative areas called dioceses. At the head of each diocese was a bishop and his administrative centre was the cathedral. It was usually the largest and most magnificent church in the diocese. Cathedrals all over Europe were built in cities because only the cities were wealthy enough to build on such a large scale. But in England there were other cathedrals, such as Canterbury, Winchester and Worcester, which were staffed by members of a religious order, such as monks, and these were often built within a monastic site rather than in a city.

Early medieval cathedrals were simple stone structures, built in a style called Romanesque because they had architectural features that were learned from the Romans. They had rounded arches on doorways and windows and a rounded

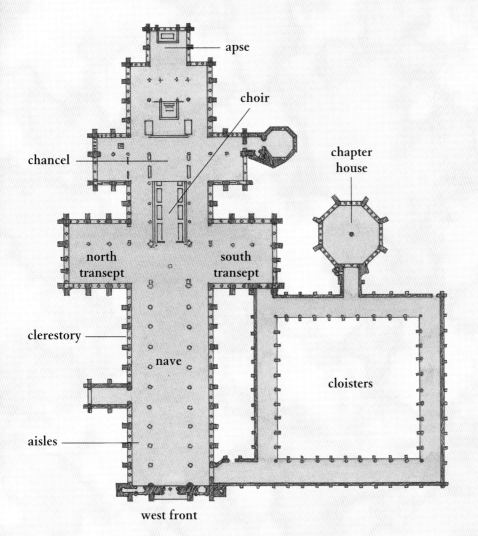

apse

choir

chancel

chapter house

north transept

south transept

clerestory

nave

cloisters

aisles

west front

This diagram shows the layout of Salisbury Cathedral, begun in 1220. At the south of the building are the cloisters, a covered walkway where monks could walk and meditate, and the chapter house where business was conducted.

A Description of Lincoln Cathedral

'With proud boldness the wall soars up towards the clouds and the roof towards the stars. The vault seems to converse with the winged birds; it spreads broad wings of its own and like a flying creature jostles the clouds … handsome jointing arranges there in seemly rank a thousand shafts which strong, precious, and gleaming render the whole structure of the cathedral durable with their strength while enriching it with their costliness … for the shafts stand soaring and lofty, their finish is clear and resplendent, their order graceful and geometrical, their beauty fit and serviceable.'
(From The Cathedral Builders of the Middle Ages, Alain Erland-Brandenburg)

chancel. These were the first cathedrals with large, high naves whose purpose was to hold a sizeable congregation of ordinary people. They were big square buildings with a chancel at the east end where the mass was said. Later in the medieval period, aisles were built along the sides of the nave for people to walk up to the altar, and a third aisle was added to cross the nave in front of the altar. Later still, side rooms called apses held smaller chapels, each with its own altar holding the sacred remains of a saint. As architects grew bolder, they built high towers for the church bell and complicated arched pillars, called clerestories, in the side walls of the nave. This style is known today as Gothic. It is characterized by a cross-shaped building, rather than a simple rectangle, and it has far more elaborate archways and pillars with lots of open spaces to let in light.

BUILDING A CATHEDRAL

Chartres Cathedral in France was begun some time in the twelfth century. Almost two hundred years later, Church officials worried that it was in danger of collapse and commissioned some architects to report on its safety:

'First: we have seen the vault of the crossing; repairs are necessary there; and if they are not undertaken ... there could be great danger.
Item: we have seen the flying buttresses; they need pointing up, and if this is not done at once damage may ensue.
Item: there are two piers which support the towers which need repairs.'
The list continues. The repairs must have been good ones, since in modern times Chartres is considered Europe's best-preserved Gothic cathedral.
(*From* Cathedral Builders of the Middle Ages)

Before a cathedral could be built, it required a patron. This was the person who commissioned the cathedral and found the money to pay for it. Kings, bishops, abbots, lords, even city councils, took on this role. Sometimes, it took hundreds of years to build a cathedral because the patron died or the cash ran out. The building of Milan Cathedral in the late fourteenth century was administered by a committee of as many as three hundred people.

After the patron, the next most important person was the architect. He drew up the plans for the cathedral and oversaw its building. Architects were often master masons, men who had learned stone masonry and sculpture as an apprentice. They travelled around Europe, learning new techniques and absorbing new styles. Later medieval architects specialized in

A great cathedral often took many years to build. The workers on the site had the use of quite complex machinery, as shown in this artist's impression of a building site.

J·E·J· MCMXCI

This fifteenth-century illustration shows a cathedral being built in Italy. Stonemasons can be seen at work, cutting up large pieces of stone.

Flying Buttresses

Architects began to discover ways of making their buildings taller and more elaborate, building wide naves with vaulted stone roofs. These buildings quickly grew beyond the point where the outer walls could support the weight of the masonry and other ways had to be found to keep the building upright. One of these was the flying buttress. This was an arched-shaped support, which stood against the outer walls of the building. By the end of the medieval age, these buttresses often had three or more tiers taking the support higher and allowing for even taller, wider buildings. Occasionally there were accidents with ceilings collapsing, such as the ceiling vault of the church of Cluny Monastery in France, which collapsed in 1120 during the building process.

just one aspect of a building – staircases or towers, for example – and several architects worked on each project.

Alongside the architect was a team of stonemasons. The masons sourced the stone, cut it themselves, made their own tools, carved the stone into the desired shapes, and set it in place. To do this they had simple winches and cranes for lifting. Scaffolding was built into the walls as the building rose upward; walkways along the scaffolding were made of woven basketwork. To accurately create the fine detail in carved pillars, patterns were drawn out on a stone or plaster floor, and the stone to be carved was set on it.

Alongside these master craftsmen were other skilled workers: carpenters, mortar mixers, blacksmiths and plasterers. Records show that skilled masons often earned twice as much as the plasterers, who in turn earned more than the unskilled manual workers, the water carriers, hod carriers, carters and general labourers.

CATHEDRAL DECORATIONS

Medieval Clocks

Mechanical clocks are a medieval invention and early ones were the most complex piece of machinery yet known. They were also extremely expensive to make and only very wealthy places, such as monasteries or cathedrals, could afford to have one. A metal face showed the time, and mechanical figures might move to strike the hours. Clocks were at first kept inside the cathedral, where only the clergy could see them, and their only function was to make sure that services were held at the right time.

Even the simplest of churches in the Middle Ages contained silver or gold objects, such as this chalice for holding the altar wine.

The medieval cathedral had no seating, heating or light, beyond candles, but it was a riot of colour, from the brightly painted walls, statues and ceilings to the huge stained glass windows.

To the east of the nave was the chancel, separated from it by an ornately carved wooden or stone screen. In the chancel was the altar. Inside this were the remains of a saint whose presence made the altar holy. The remains would have been held in a specially made container, called a reliquary, which was covered in precious stones. Many rich men gave the Church gifts in the hope of forgiveness for their sins, and so

the medieval chancel became filled with silver and gold chalices and other instruments used for the mass. Also inside the chancel were the carved and decorated bishop's throne and the stalls for the choir.

At the west end of the cathedral was the font, a carved stone basin that held holy water. Over the years, a collection of monuments and tombs accumulated around the walls of the nave. They were dedicated to the wealthy men who supported the church. They were often carved from alabaster or marble.

Unlike today, the inside walls of medieval cathedrals were plastered and brightly painted. The paintings might illustrate stories from the Bible, saints' lives, or stories that warned what would happen to sinners. The most interesting aspect of the thousands of surviving wood and stone carvings are the variety of stories to be found depicted on them. They include scenes from rural life, strange animals, human faces, even figures of the men who built the cathedral, from mortar mixers and hod carriers to the architect himself.

The outside of the cathedral was even more intricately carved than the interior. Every opportunity was taken to decorate the exterior, from gargoyles spouting rainwater down from the roof to figures of the saints over the door. The west entrance of the cathedral was always the most highly decorated. In time, even architectural features such as the flying buttresses became elaborately carved, looking more like delicate wings than supports for the walls.

A Disapproving Voice
Not everyone in the Church approved of the increasingly ornate and expensive objects which began to decorate cathedrals. Here is the opinion of one senior Church leader: 'I put on one side the vast height of the churches, the excessive length, the empty spaces, the rich finish, the curious paintings. We will look rather at the sumptuous ornaments encrusted with gems and gold, put there that money may breed money and pilgrims may give to monks the alms that should be bestowed upon the true poor.'
(From Medieval Worlds: A Sourcebook, edited by Roberta Anderson and Dominic Bellenger)

Mechanical clocks, such as this one at Wells Cathedral, England, were first constructed in Europe towards the end of the thirteenth century.

CHURCH MUSIC

Christmas Celebrations at Cluny Monastery
A quote from Peter the Venerable, twelfth-century abbot of Cluny Monastery: 'It is the custom of Cluny to celebrate the saviour's nativity with singular affection, and with more devotion than any other solemn feast; not only with melody of song, with longer lessons in church, with the light of multitudinous tapers, but far beyond all this with special devotion and copious shedding of tears, in joyful unison with the angelic Host.' (*From* Life in the Middle Ages, *G. C. Coulton*)

The earliest church music was a simple chant, known as the Gregorian chant, that accompanied religious services. The monks sang the words of the service without any other musical accompaniment. In the early part of the medieval age, the choir consisted entirely of clergymen – monks or priests employed in the cathedral.

Later, as the Gregorian chant grew more complicated, this caused problems. Monks were not always the best singers; also, they could not always be available for the service. So, by the middle of the period, the Church had begun to employ lay people (non-clergy) to sing in the choirs. Only men and boys were allowed to join the choirs. Some cathedrals and monasteries such as Rome, Metz in Germany, and St Gall in Switzerland, had choir schools where boys learned the profession. Sometimes, rivalry broke out between cathedrals over a particularly good chorister, and occasionally choirmasters resorted to kidnapping.

This fifteenth-century illustration shows a group of monks singing together. At the borders of the picture are laymen studying texts, illustrating the idea that ordinary laymen could also read the scriptures.

The bells of the village church in Saintes-Maries-de-la-Mer in southern France. The simple twelfth-century church not only has this complex set of bells, but contains holy relics said to have belonged to the Virgin Mary's sister and the mother of Saints James and John who, legend says, fled to this place in the year 40 CE.

The first organs were placed in cathedrals some time in the tenth century. They were very simple machines with levers rather than a keyboard, and were intended for use during processions to add to the grandeur of the event rather than to accompany singing. By the eleventh century, organs had keyboards and were smaller, so they could be carried to where they were needed.

It is unlikely that other musical instruments were used in the medieval church service, although cathedral decorations often include pictures of angels playing instruments. Even more curiously, there are many carvings of animals playing instruments, such as the bagpipes or the organ. This may be because the Church believed that secular music was sinful.

Another form of music was church bells. In their simplest form they were a single note, intended to tell the congregation that it was time to come to church. Early medieval bells were simple metal tubes, which were struck rather than swung. By the thirteenth century the shape of the modern bell had been invented, and people had discovered that the size and proportions of the bell determined the sound it made. This meant that several bells could be hung together to make a tune when they were rung in a certain pattern. Bell manufacture became an important trade, and bell foundries flourished.

The bells of Ely Cathedral
In the 1340s, the bells of Ely Cathedral in England were replaced and the account sent by the manufacturer to the bishop has survived. Besides the cost of the charcoal, the moulds, the labour and the rope, the account records the names and weights of the bells. Bells were given religious names and their weight recorded. A hundredweight (cwt) is equal to 51 kg and a pound (lb) is equal to 0.45 kg.
Christ - 37 cwt 92 lbs
John - 27 cwt 4 lbs
Mary - 21 cwt 41lbs
Walsyngham – 18 cwt 4 lbs

CATHEDRAL ADMINISTRATION

Cathedrals and Funerals

The funerals of powerful men, such as bishops, were conducted in the cathedrals. The coffin was covered in velvet cloth, often embroidered in gold, and was frequently topped by a wax effigy of the deceased. It was placed in the centre of the nave and surrounded by mourners dressed in black cloaks. Above the coffin was built a wooden frame, which held candles. Beside the coffin would be the bishop's vestments, or official clothes. The body would finally be laid to rest in the cathedral grounds or in the crypt. In medieval times, people believed in the Day of Judgement, when bodies would be resurrected, and so the body was prepared for that day.

The coronation of Richard I of England in 1189. This picture shows the procession on the way to the cathedral.

Medieval cathedrals were almost certainly the biggest employers of people in their regions. City cathedrals employed members of religious orders to assist the bishop in the administration of the diocese, run the cathedral school, and take part in the religious service each evening. Besides the clergy, the cathedral employed many other people to maintain the church building, carry out the day-to-day business of the church, and look after the cathedral grounds.

Monastic cathedrals were not run by bishops, but by the order to which the monastery belonged. The cathedrals formed part of highly complex communities. Besides the monks, who spent their daily lives in prayer or study, the monastery had its own land and its own serfs to farm it.

Some tithe barns, such as this one in Widdington, Essex, survive into modern times.

The Coronation of Richard I

The medieval historian, Roger of Hovedon, describes King Richard I's coronation: 'When the duke (Richard) had come to the altar, in presence of the archbishops, bishops, clergy, and people, kneeling before the altar, with the holy Evangelists placed before him, and many relics of the saints … he swore that he would all the days of his life observe peace, honour, and reverence towards God, the Holy Church, and its ordinances....

Then Baldwin, archbishop of Canterbury, pouring holy oil upon his head, anointed him king in three places, on his head, breast, and arms, which signifies glory, valour, and knowledge, with suitable prayers for the occasion.... They then clothed him in the royal robes … after which the archbishop delivered to him the sword of rule, with which to crush evildoers against the Church....'
(*From* Roger of Hoveden: The Annals)

Within each diocese were many smaller churches. Each of these churches paid tithes, or special Church taxes, to the cathedral to contribute to its upkeep. These churches, in their turn, collected tithes from their congregations. A small village church would have its own living, a farm, which provided the parish priest's income. In addition, the priest could expect to receive payments for each baptism or marriage. Many villagers paid their tithes in kind rather than cash, and there are several tithe barns still in existence which were built to hold the grain paid to the church as tithes. The parish priest was aided by one or more curates, young priests who were learning their trade and waiting to be given a parish of their own.

MONASTERIES AND ABBEYS

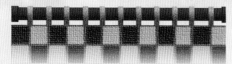

The Monastic Life
'When you wish to sleep, they wake you, when you wish to eat, they make you fast. The night is passed praying in the church, the day in working, and there is no repose but in the refectory; and what is found there? Rotten eggs, beans with their pods on, and liquor fit for oxen.'
(From Medieval Britain, *Lloyd and Jennifer Laing)*

Small numbers of monasteries had existed in Europe since the third century. With the innovations of St Benedict in the sixth century and the reforms of Pope Gregory in the eleventh century (see page 7), monasteries became more organized, and also more popular. The largest monasteries were called abbeys; smaller ones were known as priories.

Monasteries were self-contained communities, providing everything the monks or nuns required for their everyday existence. At the heart of each monastery was the abbey church. There was also a cloister, a covered passageway where inmates could study and work; a scriptorium, where manuscripts were copied, illustrated, stored or read; a kitchen and refectory; an infirmary; a school for training novice monks and sometimes lay children; a grain store; a bakehouse; workshops for blacksmiths, potters, tanners, weavers and brewers; guest accommodation; an old people's home; gardens; water mills; and a farm run by the monastery and worked on by the monks and by peasant workers.

Life was harsh in the early monasteries. The monks or nuns lived in poverty. They fasted regularly, ate no meat, and

This illustration shows medieval nuns and monks playing with a bat and ball, and not engaged in their religious duties.

enjoyed few comforts. They took vows of celibacy and spent their days and nights observing strict rituals of prayer and work. Some orders even took vows of silence. Their work might involve toiling in the fields, creating illuminated manuscripts or teaching. For hundreds of years, the monasteries were centres of art and scholarship.

By the twelfth century, monasteries had grown wealthy from donations of land and money. The large influx of ordinary people to monastic orders led to a relaxation of the rules. Meat was allowed in the diet and monks were able to employ more peasants to work the land. Monasteries kept horses, and pleasures such as hunting with hawks and, in the case of nuns, buying fashionable clothes, became common.

There were some efforts at reforming the monasteries during the twelfth and thirteenth centuries. In 1210, St Francis of Assisi founded the Franciscan order. They took their vows of poverty very seriously and were allowed no possessions. Franciscan monks, known as friars, supported themselves by working or begging for alms. However, the Franciscan movement could not halt the general decline of the monasteries. By the fourteenth century, monasteries were despised by many people as greedy landlords. Monks and friars became associated with laziness, and were ridiculed by Chaucer in *The Canterbury Tales*.

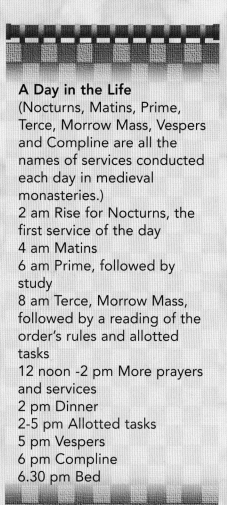

A Day in the Life
(Nocturns, Matins, Prime, Terce, Morrow Mass, Vespers and Compline are all the names of services conducted each day in medieval monasteries.)
2 am Rise for Nocturns, the first service of the day
4 am Matins
6 am Prime, followed by study
8 am Terce, Morrow Mass, followed by a reading of the order's rules and allotted tasks
12 noon -2 pm More prayers and services
2 pm Dinner
2-5 pm Allotted tasks
5 pm Vespers
6 pm Compline
6.30 pm Bed

Most monasteries had their own fields, tended to by the monks.

HOLY GROUND

Memorials

Few medieval tombs remain in today's churchyards but those inside the churches have survived. Most of these belong to distinguished members of the church or important members of society. Their memorials focus on what they had done during their life to justify being remembered. Hughes Libergies, the architect of Rheims Cathedral in France, is shown on his tombstone holding a model of the cathedral. Some are more creative. The tomb of John Stanley in Elford, England, shows him holding the tennis ball that killed him. Towards the end of the medieval age, when a terrible plague had killed hundreds of thousands of people across Europe, tombstones began to reflect an obsession with death. Tombstone carvings showed the rotting corpse that lay beneath, and inscriptions warned the living to be aware of their own impending death.

A fugitive claiming sanctuary at a cathedral door.

The grounds of the cathedral formed a special area around the church where much of the social activity of medieval life took place. In English cathedrals, the area around the church was called the close. It was a piece of open land around which the various other buildings associated with the church, such as the bishop's palace, houses for other clergymen, and the churchyard itself, were grouped. The immediate area around the church building formed the churchyard and was the burial place for ordinary citizens. In the period between 1208 and 1214, when church services were banned in England, churchmen were forbidden to conduct burials. There are stories of coffins being hung from trees in the churchyard until they could be buried later.

The churchyard had other functions besides the burial of the dead. In the churchyards of the great cathedrals, that formed part of the pilgrims' route, there were permanent stalls selling commemorative badges and flasks of holy water and oil. The

pilgrims could carry these home from their trip to show they had made the journey. Some churchyards contained high crosses engraved with scenes from the Bible, for the benefit of those who could not read. The church door, or sometimes the churchyard gate, was the site for medieval weddings.

The churchyard was also used for a number of less sacred activities. Although trading on Sundays was banned by the Pope in 906, fairs were often held in churchyards on Sundays. During All Hallows, pagan practices such as putting out food for the dead were still carried out in graveyards. May Day and Midsummer's Day in England were often celebrated by building tents of green leaves against the walls of the church and performing plays beneath them. In 1240 the authorities were forced to ban dancing at the cemetery of Worcester Cathedral in England.

For fugitives from justice, another useful part of the cathedral grounds was the sanctuary knocker on the cathedral door. Once a person reached this door and took hold of the knocker they could not be arrested.

The Black Prince
'Such as thou art, sometimes was I,
Such as I am, such shalt thou be.
I little thought on th'oure of death,
So long as I enjoyed breath.

But now a caitiffe poore am I,
Deepe in the ground, lo here I lie,
My beautie great is all quite gone,
My flesh is wasted to the bone.'

Written on the tomb of Edward, the Black Prince (1359–76), son of Edward III and heir to the English throne, at Canterbury Cathedral in England.

THE END OF AN ERA

The Black Death
In the fourteenth century, a terrible plague, known as the Black Death, spread across Europe, killing two thirds of the population. The plague caused a change in attitudes towards the Church. Some saw it as a punishment from god, and so became more religious in the hope of salvation. However, others began to question the teachings of a Church that could offer no help against the disease. Most physicians were members of the clergy, and their failure to find a cure made the Church seem powerless in a time of crisis.

For centuries, the Church dominated the arts, philosophy, architecture and science. But, as the medieval period drew to a close, new ideas began to challenge the traditional views of the Church.

Beginning in Italy in the later fourteenth century, a movement emerged, known as the humanism, inspired by the rediscovery of ancient Greek and Roman art, science and philosophy. The humanists were deeply Christian, yet they were critical of the way the Church laid so much stress on spiritual development. The humanists believed that ordinary, non-religious activities like education, business and the arts were also very important.

The humanist challenge to the Church became more serious in the mid-fifteenth century with the invention of the printing press. By 1500 about six million books had been printed in Europe. Literacy levels rose, and the Church found it increasingly difficult to maintain control over what people read, discussed and learned.

The figure of Death stands triumphantly, watching over victims of the Black Death.

With the spread of new ideas came increasingly urgent calls for reform of the Church. People were critical of its wealth and perceived corruption. To many Christians, the Church seemed more concerned with collecting tithes and selling indulgences (forgiveness for past sins in exchange for money) than looking after the souls of its people.

In 1517, Martin Luther published his criticisms of the sale of indulgences. Luther believed that forgiveness could not be bought, and that people could only be forgiven for their sins if they really felt repentance. His criticisms were published and spread quickly across Europe. The resulting controversy split the Church and led eventually to the creation of a new Christian movement, known as Protestantism, that rejected the need for a pope.

By the end of the Middle Ages, the era of the Church as a single, all-powerful insitution, dominating every aspect of people's lives, and uniting Europe under the authority of the pope, was over.

Some of Luther's Criticisms

In 1517, Luther published 95 statements concerning the sale of indulgences, which he pinned on the church door at Wittenberg, Germany. Here are some of them:

'21... those preachers of indulgences are in error, who say that by the Pope's indulgences a man is freed from every penalty, and saved;

24... the greater part of the people are deceived by that indiscriminate and high sounding promise of release from penalty.

32. They will be condemned eternally, together with their teachers, who believe themselves sure of their salvation because they have letters of pardon.

43. Christians are to be taught that he who gives to the poor or lends to the needy does a better work than buying pardons;

52. The assurance of salvation by letters of pardon is vain.'

Martin Luther (1483-1546) was a simple Augustinian monk, but his ideas led to the establishment of Protestantism.

TIMELINE

1020	Building work on Chartres Cathedral, France, begins.
1073	Pope Gregory VI's reforms of the Church.
1083–9	Building of Ely Cathedral.
1072	Lincoln Cathedral begun.
1079	Winchester Cathedral begun.
1087	St Paul's Cathedral in London burns down and rebuilding begins.
1095	Pope Urban II launches the First Crusade.
1096	Norwich Cathedral begun.
1095–9	The First Crusade.
1093	Building of Durham Cathedral begins.
1098	The monastic order called the Cistercians is founded.
1110	The earliest record of the miracle plays in England.
1120	Part of Cluny Cathedral, France, collapses.
1147–9	The Second Crusade.
1174	Canterbury Cathedral burns down and is largely rebuilt.
1187	Muslim armies capture Jerusalem.
1189	Richard I is crowned king of England.
1189–92	The Third Crusade.
1192–1235	Wells Cathedral is built.
1202-4	The Fourth Crusade.
1208–14	All religious services in England are banned by the Pope.
1210	The Franciscan order is founded.
1220	Salisbury Cathedral is begun.
1240	Dancing is banned in the cemetery of Worcester Cathedral.
1264	The festival of Corpus Christi is celebrated for the first time.
1340	Ely Cathedral commissions a new set of bells.
1347–50	The first outbreaks of the Black Death.
1358	Banquets are banned in Exeter Cathedral.
1361	The second outbreak of the Black Death.
1376	Death of Edward, the Black Prince.
1414	Jan Hus is burned at the stake.
1453	Constantinople falls to the Turks.
1478	The Spanish Inquisition begins.
1487–98	Portuguese voyages of discovery begin.
1492	Christopher Columbus discovers America.
1517	Luther publishes his criticisms of the Church.

All Souls, All Hallows Christian festivals celebrated in the autumn.

baptism A religious service in which someone, usually a baby, is officially welcomed into the Christian Church.

Byzantium The eastern section of the Roman Empire, consisting of areas of south-east Europe and Asia Minor, with the city of Constantinople as its capital.

cardinal A senior figure in the Church hierarchy, who helps to choose the new pope.

celibacy Not marrying or engaging in sex.

clergyman Someone who has taken vows to be a member of the Church.

confession A ceremony in which a parishioner tells his or her priest all the sins he or she has committed in recent days.

Corpus Christi A summer Christian festival that celebrates the belief that the body and blood of Christ are present in the mass.

corruption The use of power for an immoral purpose.

Crusades A series of military expeditions engaged in by Christians with the aim of breaking Muslim control over what was seen as the Holy Land in the Middle East.

diocese An area ruled over by a bishop.

divine right The belief that kings or emperors ruled with authority granted to them by God.

excommunication The decision by the pope to remove a person's right to take part in Holy Communion, or to continue as a member of the Church.

gargoyles Stone carvings of imaginary creatures placed over a rainwater spout on the roof of a cathedral.

heresy Religious beliefs which do not agree with those of the Church leadership.

hierarchy A system or organization in which members are arranged in ranks of authority.

Holy Communion The occasion when a Christian eats the bread and drinks the wine that represent the body and blood of Christ.

holy water Water that has been blessed by a priest.

Holy Week The week surrounding Easter Day, that commemorates the death and subsequent resurrection of Jesus Christ.

humanism A philosophy that emerged in Italy in the fourteenth century, and later spread to other parts of Europe. It emphasised the development of human virtues, such as compassion and honour; and human potential, for example in education, science and the arts.

indulgences Letters from the pope forgiving someone for their sins.

Inquisition A special court set up by the Church, composed of priests who investigated and tried people accused of heresy.

Last Judgement The Christian belief that on the last day of the earth everyone will rise from the grave and be judged by God.

mason A person who builds using stone.

mass A religious service in the Catholic Church. Bread and wine represent the body and blood of Christ and each member of the congregation eats a piece of the bread and drinks some wine.

medieval age The period of European history between the fall of the Roman empire and the fall of Constantinople in 1453.

Middle East The geographical region between Egypt and Iran.

monasticism The way of life of monks and nuns, who withdraw from society and spend their days in prayer and abstinence.

mortar A mixture of lime and sand that is used to cement stone blocks together.

mystery plays A series of plays telling the story of the life of Christ.

reliquary A container made of precious metal in which a holy relic or the remains of a saint are kept.

Roman Empire The territories ruled by Rome under its emperors, from 31 BCE to 476 CE.

sacraments Religious rituals conducted by a priest.

secular To do with the everyday life of people rather than their religious beliefs.

tithes One tenth of a person's produce that had to be given to the church each year.

winch A machine that helps to lift heavy objects.

RECOMMENDED READING

DK Eyewitness Guides: Medieval Life, Andrew Langley (Dorling Kindersley, 2002)

Life in the Middle Ages, Mark Ormrod (Wayland, 1991)

Heinemann History Series: Life in Medieval Times, Judith Kidd (Heinemann, 2001)

Medieval Britain: The Medieval Church, Peter Chrisp (Hodder Wayland, 1996)

RECOMMENDED WEBSITES

http://www.btinternet.com/~timeref
http://www.learnhistory.org.uk/medieval
http://www.britainexpress.com/where_to_go_in_Britain/cathedrals/cathedrals/.htm
http://www.learner.org/exhibits/middleages/morelign.html

Note to parents and teachers

Every effort has been made by the publishers to ensure that these websites are suitable for children, that they are of the highest educational value, and that they contain no inappropriate or offensive material. However, because of the nature of the Internet, it is impossible to guarantee that the contents of these sites will not be altered. We strongly advise that Internet access is supervised by a responsible adult.

INDEX